bottled feelings

by bella karad,
for you.

part of
Starlit dreams.

discover the whole series:
mybook.to/StarlitDreamsTheSeries

bottled feelings.

bottled feelings — bella karad

Copyright ©2023 Bella Karad

All rights reserved.

No portion of this book may be reproduced in any form without written permission from the publisher or author, except as permitted by U.S. copyright law.

ISBN: 9798856258829

bottled feelings — bella karad

contents

part 1
  loving
    pages 8 through 55

part 2
  longing
    pages 58 through 87

part 3
  crying
    pages 90 through 115

part 4
  new
    pages 118 through 128

part 1
loving

bottled feelings — bella karad

overworked and overtired
a mundane routine complete
just to start anew again
expecting nothing but the ordinary
nothing of note to happen
yet getting something special, unexpected
something—
        someone
who would become
what i never realized
i could ever have.

bottled feelings — bella karad

feelings of excitement
from just one notification
felt like it was special
from the very first hello.

bottled feelings — bella karad

i should visit was what i uttered
not even thinking
about what that entails
     a long trek
          a journey to the place
where someone i wanted
someone i needed
had been waiting
for me all along.

bottled feelings — bella karad

time flying by
as we discuss the meaning of life
emotions and regrets
the feeling that we are
made for one another
swiftly creeping
and softly settling in
many miles between us
yet just one plane ride
keeping us apart.

bottled feelings — bella karad

time is all i have.
glad to give you all of it:
it is infinite

bottled feelings — bella karad

give me your heart
and i will put it with mine
away forever
secure in a safe
the combination known
only
to us.

bottled feelings — bella karad

we were
standing
outside
in the cold
but couldn't
feel a thing.

bottled feelings — bella karad

soft as morning light,
fingers travel for miles
across earths of skin.

8:42pm

your eyes look like sunset today.

don't close them just yet.

bottled feelings — bella karad

my love,
i can think of so many
things to say to you,
but when i see you
i get tongue-tied.
and if i say what i'm thinking
it will never come out
the way i want it to.

that's what you do to me;
you affect me with your existence.

i'm sitting here,
the thought itself
is sickening;
how i love the way
you make me feel
so much

but all i do is hear you speak,
hoping that one day,
i can tell you
how much you mean to me

that my darling,
you any more than words
will ever be.

i remember the first time that you got close to me. hands in the right places along with the music in the background, feeling like it's just the two of us alone, knowing that people are surrounding us, watching our moves for the first time, witnessing our spark becoming a connection, within a moment in time. i knew that this was the purpose to feel this way, that this was meant to be. for the first time, as i was being held by you, swaying along with the music, the word *safe* was starting to make sense, i felt safe in your arms and for the first time i knew that our story would begin.

bottled feelings — bella karad

light brown, tanned skin
sun-bleached tips
and cracked lips
rough flesh touching flesh
the boy who calls himself the sun
is rugged, messy and handsome
pearly whites, dimples in his cheeks
missing a tooth, he grins at me
so bright, i can barely stand him
but something tells me that
whatever happens
he'll be there.

bottled feelings — bella karad

you were like music,
and i longed to dance.

your heart was the beat,
and i begged for a chance.

your words were the vocals,
and i was put in a trance.

your smile was the melody,
and i fell in love at first glance.

bottled feelings — bella karad

i touched your soul
and scribbled my name on it.
love, you'll never get lost again.

bottled feelings — bella karad

she had galaxies
in her eyes
and her tears
were falling stars.

bottled feelings — bella karad

pull you close
grab my waist
rest my hands
on your face
kiss you slow
close embrace
lift me up
wearing lace
hands will drift
press and trace
melting with
the sweet taste
of love on our lips
and time to waste
you and i
in this place.

bottled feelings — bella karad

you're the past i craved for,
the present i adore,
the future i want.
i love you.

bottled feelings — bella karad

and for you,
my heart swells like a new moon,
it beats like the sun
at one o'clock in the afternoon.
and my blood rushes,
gushes, like a warm winter shower;
my eyes gleaming,
like a dewy spring flower.

bottled feelings — bella karad

if you are the ocean
then i am the mist
that kisses the morning
the way i'd want
to be kissed

if you are the ocean
then anchors aweigh
we'll sail through the evening
and on to the light
the daystar is dawning
we'll keep to the right

like peter and wendy
to neverlands' door
we'll sail on forever
and touch every shore

if you are the ocean,
come wash me away
to some misty morning
and there we will play

if you are the ocean,
then sing me a song
of sailors and treasures
and places long gone

if you are the ocean
come wash me away
to a place, together we'll
forever stay...

bottled feelings — bella karad

happiness
is just part of our journey.
unconditional love,
undying commitment
will make it last.

bottled feelings — bella karad

there is art
in your heart
painting pictures
when i lay
my head down on your chest

there are songs in your eyes
singing lullabies
when you hover
pinning me down
with your stare

there is a poem
on the tip
of your tongue
i taste it
when i kiss you

bottled feelings — bella karad

please, look at me.
look at me in every way that love feels,
then peer into me as if you are meeting
a candle light to blow its heat.
   i promise i won't speak unless you need me to,
so look at me in every possible way
if it helps you see me better.

deep in your gaze,
mesh me in every memory that makes you cry
   for i am a home for dark things too.
your every spill cannot flood
the vast space of my nothingness.
   i have all the room in the world
   to take in every version of you.

my skin was off the first time i met you and you saw how ugly it was to be me. even if i looked frightening, your face remained static—you wore the kind of skin that reminded me of the most calm and quiet period of the night where i can just be myself. there, i could wear any skin i want, to hide, to be happy, to be at peace or perhaps i wear them at random just so i can feel something.

you stood there and perceived me beyond this paper skin as if my ugliness was something that can be erased. but just like every skin that is hanging inside my closet, every single one of them is threaded with some sort of deficiency and each time i wear them, i light myself on fire because i like watching myself burn. slowly, you walked towards me to warm yourself.

bottled feelings — bella karad

looking into your eyes,
i see the stars shine.

looking into your eyes,
eases my tainted mind.

looking into your eyes,
i see the love you have for mine.

your eyes are looking into mine,
i'm losing track of time.

these moments feel like forever,
i only wish they would be.

the notion that one day you won't be gazing into my eyes, makes these moments all the more special. life moves fast. enjoy the small moments. nothing in this world, is made to last. i'll be looking into your eyes, i hope that sight will be my very last.

bottled feelings — bella karad

there's something about the sea:
in feeling a force of nature
so much stronger than yourself,
surround you in its embrace.

there's something about the waves,
their raw power,
their cool, demanding strength.

and there's something about his hands,
his voice, his eyes.
the way his body pulls mine under,
like waves,
indomitable, forceful,
alive.

and i'm floating.
i'm sinking.
i'm thrown around in the current.
in his arms: the sea;
the breath he steals
then grants it back.

and i pray only
that the tide never subsides.

bottled feelings — bella karad

i never thought i would discover a passion as yourself. miracles restore my desolated mind, repeating a problematic past. the demons no longer reach me with their screams, the damage done to my spirit, it all vanishes from your embrace. your voice is the loveliest tune in the world. i would rather not live without the colors your mind paints into life. music sings and fills the air from your soul. you know enough about yourself, still, it's a mystery to you. blessings are bestowed upon us, upon all from your divine presence. it's remarkable. it's astonishing. vibrantly godly. without you, i would not be able to dream.

bottled feelings — bella karad

night falls in waves of dark cerulean
again, i am taken by the thought of you
time must move slow
at the way my mind thinks you through

a love song plays its sweet tune
distant compared to my desire
slowly we move
dancing to the beat of our burning fire

feelings grow strong
grounded and stable
you plant the seed of romance in my heart
bounds of emotion becoming fatal

i yearn for your affection
sweet— the taste on my tongue
your sybaritic words filling me up
and to you, i clung

my words mean not only of sexual desire
be clear in knowing i want it all
we can be spoiled in platonic pleasure
and in you, i will fall.

bottled feelings — bella karad

it just hit me:
i want to string beautiful words along just for you,
only to imagine you smiling as you read them.
as i think them, i ponder about you and it sinks in:
i'd fill myself up with honey and let you drink me
if only that would make you feel me.

how would i be in your throat?
golden, shiny and liquid?

gently dripping from your chin,
shimmering and
exquisite.

bottled feelings — bella karad

fire burning red hot.
who will be the next to burn?
ignite a soul and light the way.
okay. now it's your turn.

in my mind like spring time.
dew drops steam off of the soft
flowers they became upon.
i evaporate to high skies from
the ground i'm standing on.

something of a bad bliss.
i stumble into your forbidden kiss
and i feel like myself again.

for i am no saint.
these words may be faint.
but to you, i'd lend my hand again.
it's you who i will lay again,
in the dangerous alley ways
of my hidden places.

and when you come looking,
just search in the shadows.

this is where i'll meet you.

bottled feelings — bella karad

people change everyday.
so i vow to fall in love with you
every time the moon sets and the sun rises.

bottled feelings — bella karad

dream of me
i am real.
i am where smiles are made
and tears fade away
where hope springs forth
away from the darkness
of the earth

i am the glow of the moon
and all the stars in the sky
those who seek the light
shall have me as their guide

i am the red bird or butterfly you see
just keep your eyes open... to find me
i am where tomorrow is coming
and hope always holds on

my darling,
i am never truly gone...

bottled feelings — bella karad

lick my lips
cradle my face
gaze into my eyes
and tell me i'm safe.

bottled feelings — bella karad

in your eyes
i wanna drown

in your lips
i wanna melt

in your warmth
i wanna die

and in your arms
i wanna be buried.

bottled feelings — bella karad

there,
under barely any light,
i find art within your eyes,
as like stars are found in the night's sky,
you're a masterpiece no darkness can hide.

bottled feelings — bella karad

and you are
just like the moon
— so, alone —
but you shine bright
at the darkest
of times.

bottled feelings — bella karad

i find myself... thinking
about you;
sunsets,
beautiful lyrics

in the sound of
thunder,
in the calm
of soft rain, drizzling

in all the little things
and inside the
deepest part
of my soul.

bottled feelings — bella karad

    as passion surrounds me in the dark
hearts ignited into a spark.
tongues mate, a ritual dance
lost in a bliss without a chance.
    the gentle caress upon my face
tingling sensations grow with the trace
in a frenzy of kisses long denied
hungered passion can no longer hide.
    within this depth we are deeply drawn
as sensual desires begin to spawn
night passion is lost in endless time
as i become drunk on your sensual wine.
    tender kisses placed upon my skin
no fighting desires that i can't win
my soul and heart fly as you caress
slowly, slowly as we undress
    heat deepens into our senses
passion tearing into our defenses
your kissing lips move upon my leg
sending silent urges as i beg
    longing boils and starts to crest
as we glide into our quest.
while we lay our bodies intertwine
intoxicating me with your sensual wine.
    trembles quake, ecstasy takes control
whimpers escape my lips, as you caress my soul.
desire drips, sweat runs down your back
drawn into passion as our souls attack.
    slowing from our quicken pace
gentle kisses rain upon my face
a blissful aftermath, i'm lost in time
from being drunk on our sensual wine.

bottled feelings — bella karad

i like to say
your name
when you're
not here
turn you
into sound
conjure you out of
thin air
so that you appear
before me
dressed in sound
only
memory sketching in
the rest of you
as if sound
was just an outline
and love
colors you in
adding the voice last
so i can hear you say
hello you!
and there you are
as present
as present can be.
i like to say
your name
when you're
not there.

bottled feelings — bella karad

of one thing i am sure and that is that i am unsure of myself, and it's funny how i can't sleep, but my chest closes its eyes and hums with a heartbeat that is unsure of itself, too. i try to morph into a body i don't feel belongs to me, just so i can fit in somewhere. and i tell so many stories about the universe, it forever feels like i'm trying to remain lost.

i am unsure of myself; connecting the moles on my skin as if they will spell out something bigger, so i can feel like i matter, at least for a little while. i sleep beside myself, stare at a reflection so unfamiliar, i couldn't even identify it in a crowd of strangers, but i am trying. and one day i'm sure i'll be sure of myself, but until then, i'll morph into someone i can be proud of, and hope that the universe sends me back to myself.

bottled feelings — bella karad

slipping past my bones
deeply over the rim

nightfall liquid rushing
through the crown
of my head
eyes wide, aglow
   with new vision

yes. i will meet you there
in subconscious phosphorescence
pools of knowledge
forming between
the feather weight
of our lashes

wait for me
for i am floating
stellar-dipped arms
outstretched,
feeling the particles
the soft space between
our eyes, aligned

come
let us receive each other
in astral ease
a rocking delight
of non-physical
until we can one day

touch.

bottled feelings — bella karad

as beauty kisses
the dark of night
dreams of whispers
take heavenly flight,
floating high, above sleepy beds
leaving whispering dreams
to fall
upon
sleepy heads...
so dream
a dream,
of your love so true
while stars twinkle
silver and blue...
as mr. moon
watches from above
the most beautiful dreams
of sweetest love...

bottled feelings — bella karad

the gleaming moonshine on your hair,
fragmented star splitters in your eye,
your smile repainting supernova's glare
appoint you the ruler of my sky.

bottled feelings — bella karad

if i were to write a one-word poem,
i'd write your name.

bottled feelings — bella karad

the sky is a mellow orange and my heart is fuller than it's ever been. an overwhelming sense of gratefulness washes over me like the waves onto the sand. looking over at you, i realize that, in this moment, i have everything i've ever wanted, everything i've ever worked for. i am finally content with who i am and where i am. life is still messy, but it's perfect. it's authentic and it's beautiful. and there's nothing else i need but to sit here with you, listening to soft songs and soaking up the smell of the trees mixed with the ocean breeze.

bottled feelings — bella karad

having him by my side
 makes me feel safe
  from all the dangers
   that i may come across
    during this walk in life.
    with him by my side
     i feel capable to walk
      these paths life puts before me,
      i know that all steps
       i walk by his side
        will be worthy ones
         they will be the right ones.
          because i feel his strength of love
           decency
            friendship
             honesty
              faithfulness
               by the simple touch of his hand
               and
                by the light in his eyes
                 when he looks at me.
                  he helps me look to the future
                   with a certainty
                    that happiness is possible
                     those obstacles
                      we should never fear,
                       there will always be obstacles
                        always dark clouds and shadows
                         but
                          together, we will always find a way
                           out of these difficulties
                            we together will always find our light.

bottled feelings — bella karad

because we together
 will always keep our hearts
  filled with this greater feeling
  called love.
   a love that means unity
    harmony, companionship
     and
      faith
       in a life, we have chosen
        together.
         for our hearts
          are filled with a beauty
          and
           inflated with the confidence
           and hope
            only a great love can bring.

bottled feelings — bella karad

i still remember
  how i smiled
    how i giggled
      how i daydreamed
about us
the night i got back
from our first date.

bottled feelings — bella karad

my heart is so full of you
i can hardly call it my own.

part 2
longing

bottled feelings — bella karad

loving you is torture
should i keep on
swimming toward you
can i keep my
head over water
do i
drown

bottled feelings — bella karad

is this
what it feels like
to be a fossil
in the making?
to have pebbles,
sand and grit
swept slowly
on top of me.
not to mention
the crushing
and deafening
of miles of water
pressing it all down
to bury me.

but sometimes
sometimes there's
relief and light
when someone
digs through the
weight to reveal
the shadow of the
creature that once
laid there.
but then that husk
is reduced to
cinders in a mountain
of others.

bottled feelings — bella karad

i never realized
how easy it could be
to lose yourself—

i stopped taking time for myself,
gave myself to others,
piece by piece.

every time i put the puzzle back together,
another piece was missing.
or perhaps stolen.

one day i will no longer exist.

bottled feelings — bella karad

it's simple

never
make
    the
one
    you
love
    feel
forgotten.

bottled feelings — bella karad

lusting
is not
loving

flirting
is not
listening

touching
is not
feeling

unless,
  lusting
    flirting
      touching
are enabled by a
keen desire to love unconditionally.

bottled feelings — bella karad

i poured myself
inside your cup
pretended to be tea
your lips pursed to the rim
burning kiss
bile churns
you forgot
i'm made of sins.

bottled feelings — bella karad

you took the
easy route
with her
instead
of the long
way home
with me.

bottled feelings — bella karad

i have to forget.

that's all i can do
if i want to be anything
like i used to.

when i was whole,
when my heart was in one piece.

a few months before
your careless love destroyed me.

bottled feelings — bella karad

when i close my eyes—
i see him—
in the eternal darkness
behind my rational thoughts and emotions—
he appears from nowhere and grasps my hand—
and it feels like forever again.

bottled feelings — bella karad

we can look past his lies,
but not at the ugly truth?

bottled feelings — bella karad

i'll always smile
when i think
about you.
your soft touch,
your sweet smile,
your gentle laughter
you give me hope;
hope about people
and about society.
our paths crossed
for only a short while
but you made my
heart flutter,
you caught me
in a way i'll always
remember.

bottled feelings — bella karad

i kept chasing
you, as if
you were
a distant dream.
but dreams
are not always
dreams.
sometimes, we have
nightmares too.

bottled feelings — bella karad

i'm jealous of the rain.
it gets close to you
closer than i ever will;
it touches your skin
it combs your hair
it comes when you're sad
it stays when you're happy.
i love you but you don't love me
so i say
i'm jealous of the rain.

bottled feelings — bella karad

i can't sleep
every time i remember your words
they snap and recoil
and hurt me awake
next time when someone
promises me forever
i'll just smile
look them in the eyes and ask
how long is forever to you?

bottled feelings — bella karad

don't tell me i'm pretty
tell me that i'm passionate
that i have drive
tell me that i make you laugh
that i know how to make your day better
don't tell me i seem nice
tell me that i'm kind and compassionate
tell me that i'm not afraid to dream and to dream big
don't tell me i'm perfect
tell me the you love me despite my flaws
that you want to spend the rest of your life with me
don't tell me i'm beautiful
tell me that you'll be faithful and forever true.

bottled feelings — bella karad

you see,
that's the problem
with being the strong one
who always offers others
a hand.
everyone thinks that you
don't need a hand and
they think you have lots
of surplus energy and no
worries.

bottled feelings — bella karad

in your absence
i immersed myself in sadness,
for there was nothing left to love
in the remaining pieces of you
that was too blurry for me
to comprehend in the first place.
    was it really you?
because i felt too many heartaches
trying to filter your name in my palms
—you made me figure out
so many things on my own
as if this kind of mystery
will compel me to draw closer to you.

but i, too, am human
i grow weary of repetitive things
that remain obscure,
just like how your name
sounded sweet every time
    only for it to mean nothing to me.

like dirty laundry, my sadness
piles on top of one another,
and now i am grieving
because your name sounds like a metal
being dragged on the ground
—a heaviness that keeps
tugging my heart wide open.

there is no more room for you here,
my love for you has finally died.

bottled feelings — bella karad

he was a meteorite
that night.
she was a lamb.

not innocent, but soft.

he didn't know
he was such a meteorite, though
hurtling through her pasture,
blazing out her sky,
raining down sweet fire,
upon her winter coat.

she ate it up.

wanting nothing more
than his meteor heat on her throat.

bottled feelings — bella karad

i crave love,
a gentle touch,
a stare full of emotion
i crave passion and
desire
depth and fire
i crave an honest feeling
and haven't found it
yet
it is so absorbing that
i can't think straight
my mind is preoccupied
with a craving of love

bottled feelings — bella karad

what if i were in love with you?
what inside your world would it change?
because for me, it gives such a different view.

for me, you make appearances when i sleep,
and i don't know if it's my imagination
or if it's you trying to speak.

i know that you live just down the street-
you probably never even think about it,
but i always wonder whether we'll meet.

so, what if i were in love with you?
it might explain why you're always inside my mind.
why you seem to be lost in there—
stuck in a maze, or you were leaving it,
but left something behind.

i know that right now you're with someone;
with someone who's kind.
you seem really happy.
i know that love like that can be hard to find.

so, what if i were in love with you?
there is nothing for me to do-
i'm embarrassed enough
and i'm tormented, too.

bottled feelings — bella karad

it's funny how i'm flying high
until your words bring me down.
the truth that you speak?
it cuts deep.
i wish i was blissfully in ignorance instead.

can we go back to the days?

when i was still a mystery
that you were so eager to unravel.
when i invoked a sense of awe within you.
when you cherished every fibre of my being.
when your eyes sparkled as they found me.
when your fingers relished
as they touched my bare skin.

now we are just hollow.
and your fire has dimmed.

was it me that took it out?

yet even after all we've been through.
i still long for you.

bottled feelings — bella karad

they'll dance in our skin
make love in our scars

to the sounds of our sin
beneath fallen stars

they'll swim in our dreams
in a home with no doors

drowning as they spin
circling the rotten floors

and as lovers we die,
as lovers we die—

for how little we lived
as lovers we die

you and i,
forever together.

bottled feelings — bella karad

you know that it hurts
when your kiss lands on my cheek.
my heart explodes—
with you, i'm a fool; i'm weak.
you know how i wish
to embrace you whole. i seek
your burning passion
not friendship.
it's irrational
and selfish.
i hold myself back
as my heart falls to pieces,
when your touch ceases,
and everything hurts...
kiss me where it hurts,
kiss my everything,
love my everything,
just as i love yours.

bottled feelings — bella karad

i don't want to talk to him.
i   want to talk to him.
 don't   talk to him.
i don't want   him.
i   want   him.
              talk to him.
i.   him.
i   want   to.
i don't.

bottled feelings — bella karad

on the train to our future
hand in hand
rings meeting, polish chipped

there's many other people
some even staring
but to me
there's no one but us.

moment so safe
yet moment so short.

embracing you warmly
it never crossed my mind
that your stop would be
our last goodbye.

bottled feelings — bella karad

i miss you i texted
only to be destroyed
me too
but i'm sorry.
things could've been different
if i were okay.

bottled feelings — bella karad

how did someone
who made me feel so intensely in love
become someone
who made me scared of ever loving again?

how does someone
who i have the happiest memories with
become someone
who i wish to never think about again?

how can someone
who used to tell me i'm his everything
become someone
who doesn't think i'm enough?

how?

bottled feelings — bella karad

how could you expect me
to dive into your heart
when the water is shallow?

bottled feelings — bella karad

you used to always say
it takes you a week to miss someone.

so here i am
a week later
praying you'll tell me you miss me.

but nothing.

bottled feelings — bella karad

you were the sun
lately, all you do is
burn
my skin.

part 3
crying

bottled feelings — bella karad

only miles away
yet different sides of the globe
we could've made it
if we would've known
how much it would hurt
both of our souls
to never see each other again.

bottled feelings — bella karad

numb and hopeless
re-reading every exchange
thinking of what
i could've done differently
to keep you from what you did

now you're only a memory
someone i'll keep in my heart
for longer than i had them
here
by my side.

bottled feelings — bella karad

i'll write you music
i used to tell you
when we would just
spend our days in bed

and i did write it
though not in the way i meant
each song's title
one of your last four texts

bottled feelings — bella karad

pecking my cheek
stay safe you told me
i promised i will
and *i'll send you a text*

the text i sent said
i arrived safely
to which for years
you haven't said anything back.

bottled feelings — bella karad

i spend my days
pouring myself into the cups of others

only to find that
when it's time for myself
to take a sip

all that's left
in my cup
is the remainder of a girl
who gave too much.

bottled feelings — bella karad

a winter so harsh
that even the mighty sun
turned a little cold.

like icarus
i was too close
and felt too much
  flew
    too
      high
and burned
  a w   a   y
and now
  there is nothing left
    but
      dust.

bottled feelings — bella karad

i'll hurt myself
before you get
another chance
to hurt me.

bottled feelings — bella karad

sometimes
i can't help feeling
this is the dream,
the one where i relive
my entire life,
just before i die.

bottled feelings — bella karad

in silence
diamond drop shaped tears
falling down.
sparkling the cheeks
the child sits down on the floor.
in the silence of the dark.
an innocent little one in pain.

bottled feelings — bella karad

it's 3 am

i'm on the phone
no one's awake and i'm alone

it's 3 am

the radio's on
songs are played on lonely stations

it's 3 am

i'm in my bed
my eyes are open and sleep has fled

it's 3 am

i'm on the balcony
the sky is dark and just quite scary

it's 3 am

some windows have lights
could they also not sleep tonight?

it's 3 am

i'm still awake
when will life ever give me a break?

bottled feelings — bella karad

seeing you
makes me
miss you
more.

i'm tired.
tired of everything.
i just want to sleep,
and never wake up again.

no, i'm not lazy,
i'm not running away from life.
i'm just tired of the world and myself,
and too tired to change anything.

bottled feelings — bella karad

i just want to be forgotten
so no one has to hurt when i say
goodbye

bottled feelings — bella karad

i broke my heart again,
because i thought, finally,
i'll stop being used by you.

bottled feelings — bella karad

i'm waiting for you
to save me
from drowning
but seems like
you just wanna let go
and watch me
sink.

bottled feelings — bella karad

i'm lost
i don't know the time
i'm sitting here in the dark
going through my past
i see you
but you aren't mine.

bottled feelings — bella karad

in a drop of you,
i lost an ocean of me.

bottled feelings — bella karad

i still remember the day you took my hand,
kissed my forehead,
and told me you didn't love me.

bottled feelings — bella karad

i despise myself
for not being
someone
you could love.

bottled feelings — bella karad

days like this,
i want to walk away
from my body
forever.
i'm sure i look fine.

bottled feelings — bella karad

why was i given
such a perfect love
then had it so cruelly
taken away?

bottled feelings — bella karad

sadness
is the water filling my lungs
and flooding my throat.

bottled feelings — bella karad

with or without you,
i am alone.

bottled feelings — bella karad

i still can't sleep at night
because you wander
across my eyelids,
but this
you'll never know.

bottled feelings — bella karad

maybe
i'll be better
tomorrow.
maybe.

part 4
new

bottled feelings — bella karad

yesterday i cried to the moon
as she wiped my tears away
made my worries disappear
so i could sleep again.

today i smile at the sun
and it shines back on me,
what a wonderful world
to be alive;
to be me.

bottled feelings — bella karad

you owe
no one
your forgiveness.

except yourself.

bottled feelings — bella karad

while lilies are asleep
her dream has taken its wings
a promise of spring.

bottled feelings — bella karad

beauty of nature
everything in harmony
the blossom can't wait
to become a flower
to show her colors
to attract the bees.

bottled feelings — bella karad

sometimes,

what we know
may not be so.

what we want
may not be good for us.

what happens
may not be what we expected.

we may believe
our blessings are being blocked

when really the block
could be the blessing
we're seeking

we must learn
to bend like the trees.

bottled feelings — bella karad

i wonder if
there's ever been
a moment when
all seven billion hearts
beat in unison.

bottled feelings — bella karad

sometimes we're caught in a storm
waves crashing all around
and we forget that we can swim
we don't have to drown.

bottled feelings — bella karad

a piece of my heart will always belong to him,
no matter what.

i am not bitter.
i am not upset.

he loved me the way he knew how to love,
and isn't that beautiful?

bottled feelings — bella karad

i have sunsets on my cheeks.
blushing roses
and pinks.
i have flowers in my hair.
blooming, growing with me.
i am a wanderer
around my life.
navigating
who i am
and who i want to be.
i wonder what
the seed of the maple knew
before he was told
to be a tree.

bottled feelings — bella karad

it's been a while since i've thought about love.
i closed myself off to it,
and have yet to open up that door.

but i think about it now.
that must count for something,
or maybe nothing.
but it's on my mind.

love is a vulnerable place,
so intimate,
it's hard to find.
made impossible to search for,
behind the door.

the one i closed.
because i was too scared of the unknown.

but i have hope that i'll open it again one day.

i'll take it one day at a time.

bottled feelings — bella karad

i used to think about you
moon out or sun shining
though time has helped me heal

now you come to me
just every now and then
—whenever i feel
that i need a reminder
of what it's really like:

that you'd still be here
if i were enough.

thank you for reading,
i love you.

part of
starlit dreams.

discover the whole series:
mybook.to/StarlitDreamsTheSeries

bottled feelings.

Printed in Great Britain
by Amazon